THE DEAD PEASANT'S HANDBOOK

BRIAN TURNER

THE PEAS H BOO

ALICE · JAMES
books that matter

ALICE JAMES BOOKS
New Gloucester, ME
alicejamesbooks.org

CELEBRATING 50 YEARS
OF ALICE JAMES BOOKS

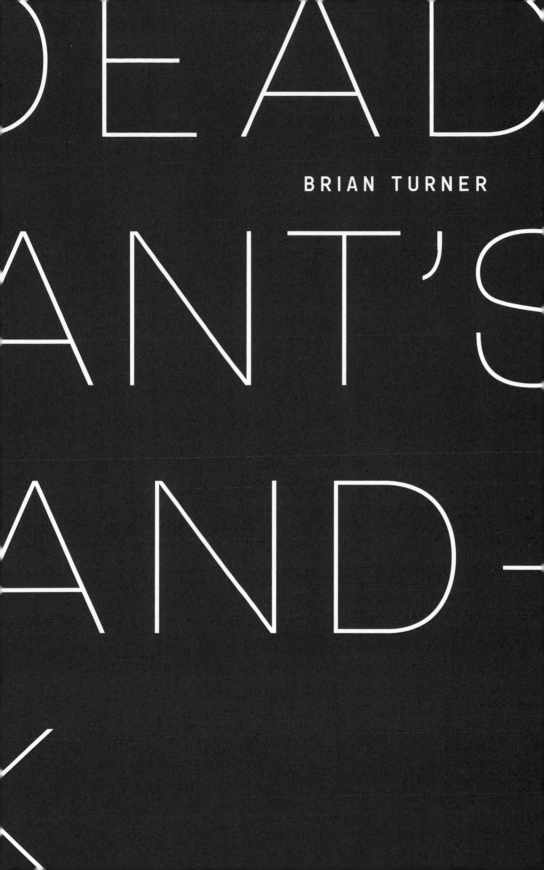

DEAD
ANT'S
AND

BRIAN TURNER

10 9 8 7 6 5 4 3 2 1

Alice James Books are published by Alice James Poetry Cooperative, Inc.

Alice James Books
Auburn Hall
60 Pineland Drive, Suite 206
New Gloucester, ME 04260
www.alicejamesbooks.org

Library of Congress Cataloging-in-Publication Data

Names: Turner, Brian, 1967- author.
Title: The dead peasant's handbook / by Brian Turner.
Description: New Gloucester, ME : Alice James Books, 2023.
Identifiers: LCCN 2023018358 (print) | LCCN 2023018359 (ebook)
 ISBN 9781949944556 (trade paperback) | ISBN 9781949944297 (epub)
Subjects: LCGFT: Poetry.
Classification: LCC PS3620.U763 D43 2023 (print) | LCC PS3620.U763 (ebook)
 DDC 811/.6—DC23/eng/20230508
LC record available at https://lccn.loc.gov/2023018358
LC ebook record available at https://lccn.loc.gov/2023018359

Alice James Books gratefully acknowledges support from individual donors, private
foundations, the National Endowment for the Arts, and the Amazon Literary Partnership.

Cover Photo: "11. Horse Croc" from *Equus* by Tim Flach

"The Call Across the Valley of Not-Knowing" from *The Book Of Nightmares*
by Galway Kinnell. Copyright © 1971 by Galway Kinnell. Used by permission of
HarperCollins Publishers.

CONTENTS

The littlest birds sing the prettiest songs.

—JOLIE HOLLAND

— I —

ON WAR & CONFLICT

SUNFLOWERS

What they don't tell you about war
is how much a bank ledger

might shape a decision tree.
The price of fuel. Sunflower oil. Durable

goods when they're floating on an ocean
with no delivery in sight. That

bullets can skip along the surface of a wall
like stones over water.

That it's a bad idea to tape the sheet glass
windows of your home, but smart

to roll down the windows of a car
when fleeing a firefight. That

you should open your mouth
to avoid rupturing your eardrums

when a shockwave rolls by. That
civilians are the bravest of all.

See how they face the invaders, saying
Take these seeds and put them in your pockets,

so at least sunflowers will grow
when you all lie down here.

What they don't tell you about war
is that a soldier's oath is not only

to be the one who puts out the fire, but
to be the one who starts the fire

to begin with, to be the one
who carves a hollow center

deep into the word *suffering*. War
is born of the obscene,

a disfiguration of words like *love*
or *humanity*. This much we know.

These things we do. These ghosts
we live with. How they call out to us

sometimes, asking for water. Such
a simple thing. A glass of water.

THE BODIES

The bodies lie along the shoulder of the road.

The bodies lie in an ambulance, a truck bed, a stretcher.

The bodies are strobed in flaring lights, color of fire, color of night.

The bodies rest within the fuselage of a plane at 36,000 feet.

The bodies contemplate silence as they wait in the morgue.

The bodies are moved from room to room, one hour to the next.

The bodies are bathed by strangers and by those who love them.

They are numbered and recorded with signatures and stamps.

They are forgotten by all save those who love them.

They are left to the fields, to the green embrace of earth.

They are given sunlight and storm, a shadow of wings descending.

They are given to rivers, to fire, to ash on the wind-driven rain.

They are carried on the shoulders of stone-faced men.

They are serenaded with tears, with the instruments of suffering.

They are eulogized in great halls and within the confines of loneliness.

They are lowered into the ground and into the vaults of memory.

They are disassembled and disbursed by the steady labor of time.

They learn more about compassion as they are lifted in someone's arms.

They learn more about the sacred as voices call around them.

They learn more about grieving as their eyes are sewn shut.

The bodies are moved from room to room, one hour to the next.

The bodies are numbered and recorded with signatures and stamps.

The bodies are bathed by strangers and by those who love them.

The bodies contemplate silence as they await the mortician, and

they are forgotten by all save those who loved them.

TWELVE ROSES FOR THE DEAD

The militia kick a soccer ball
in the street. Young men. Graybeards.
Rifles, heavy weapons. Stories. Laughter.
Their shivering hands boil coffee
in a tin over a crude fire. The buildings
no longer buildings. Landscapes of rubble
given to howling when a storm comes in.

The cease-fire will be announced soon, and
the fighting will resume until the deadline.
A vital rail line must be captured, or defended.
Or perhaps a sympathetic town must be liberated.
In high-rise offices somewhere far away, architects
design new orphanages, new hospitals, maybe
a mausoleum to be placed in a cemetery
as a way to honor the dead.

There is too much good work to be done.
Lists of provocations, demands. Diplomatic teams
negotiating in distant cities, flashbulbs ringing.
And so the militia oil their bolts, check their radios.
They smoke their last cigarettes and fall in line.
It will take hours to reach the front. Enough time
to consider the smoke drifting over the treetops,
that grim dark grove of chestnuts marching
toward the horizon before them.

And the dead woman lying on the roadside
as they pass by? She continues to be dead,
perfecting the task, though not one soul
stops or offers her the slightest bit of help.

CALL IT LEAVES AND RAIN

I was walking through the middle of my life. Walking down Divisadero Street wearing old desert combat fatigues, listening to the antifreeze boil over. I was listening to the antifreeze boil over in conversations on the street, that dead-end steaming hiss of radiators run a hundred thousand miles and more. The radiators boiled over in fatigue while I was walking a hundred thousand miles down Divisadero Street in Fresno, and it was July, and the asphalt was speaking its vapor, and I was wearing combat boots and walking through the middle of my life.

I was listening to WAR. I was listening to WAR on Divisadero Street and learning how to ride low through the rest of my life, learning how to walk the blocks in tighter and tighter circles, the way the lost do. In tighter and tighter circles, I was lost to the WAR on Divisadero Street. I was circling the WAR the way vapor curls from the steaming hiss of dead radiators in Fresno. I was circling the lost in Fresno, wearing my combat boots worn down a hundred thousand miles and counting.

And I was counting. I counted each dying face passing by. I counted the birds with their exhausted voices. I counted the sentinel birds perched silent in the eucalyptus trees above. I circled the eucalyptus birds and listened for their medicine, the way the lost do in Fresno, wearing combat boots and speaking in vapor. I was circling through the middle of my life, right there under the medicine trees, listening to the silence of the sentinel birds and waiting for them to boil over in steam. But that's not what medicine birds do.

Medicine birds break open in orange and red. Medicine birds have eucalyptus leaves for feathers and bandage the air when they fly. They fly through the windows in the head, impervious to glass. They are impervious to WAR and hiss and steam and vapor and combat and the circling lost. Medicine birds fly through the windows to land in our beds when we're dreaming our circling dream of Divisadero and Fresno with its lost and circling WAR. They have eucalyptus wings and when they fly into our beds they transform themselves into leaves and rain and lovers. The lovers in our beds are eucalyptus birds flying medicine through the windows in our heads. The lovers in our beds fly eucalyptus through the circling loss. The lovers in our beds bring medicine to our lips and call it eucalyptus, call it love, call it leaves and rain for our exhausted souls.

HISTORIANS

What they don't tell you about war
is how it outlives us. Or, how they get it wrong,

framing each war in parenthesis, like stonecutters
in the graveyards of memory, as if war isn't inscribed

into our DNA, then handed down, one generation
to another. And how we often don't learn, even so. The way

thermobaric weapons ignite the air in a cloud of plasma

and the buildings, still standing, stare at us,
their blown-out windows mouthing, *Goodbye, Goodbye.*

And what happens to the ghosts? Or the parents
with flowers at the graves of their children? Tell me,

please, how yesterday's moving oratory
might somehow replace an arm or a leg or a heartbeat.

That's what they don't tell you about war.
And I'm thinking about how it all comes home.

The way it sleeps. The way it dresses up the police
in its hand-me-downs, its assault rifles, ghillie suits,

armored personnel carriers. How the assassination of Kennedy
brought more bullhorns and nightsticks, body armor,

face shields, grenade launchers. Quick-knock and no-knock
warrants to follow, then Cold War military equipment

under Bush, while Clinton's surplus gear was made free—
so long as the police paid shipping and handling.

It's true. What they don't tell you is how Death
comes hunting for the souls of those we love,

as well as our own. What they don't tell you
is how addictive its adrenaline is, its compulsion,

or how the old vets sometimes long for a *good* war,
something that feels right. And how beautiful it can be,

sometimes, truth be told. That strange narcotic, that
pathology: war. How sweet its noxious

fumes, pluming. How it deepens the lavender
of sunsets around the globe. And that burning

of night into day, a city on fire, the mind's way
of reconstructing a neighborhood

from the ruins and the rubble. The silence after.
The years and decades of that silence. The way

it lingers in the body. Lingers on the tongue.
The way something is given wholly

to the air. It's the air. Something drifting
on the air. The way a breeze lifts it from our tongues

on a blue day in summer, say, and carries it all away.

HORSES

At 17 hands, their high-traction shoes clatter on the asphalt
as they canter forward, snorting, Perspex face shields a clear armor
for their wild-eyed vision of Molotov cocktails, stones, hurled debris,
the adrenaline of the boulevard ringing in the horns of their ears,
reflective shin guards glinting above mid-cannon and coronet, blare
of flashbulbs cracking the night open in a pure shock of light,
illuminating the signature of blaze and star on forehead and nose
as polycarbonate batons sing past their stiffened ears before they wheel
and turn, the bootheels of officers digging in, spurring their flanks,
the curtains of their lips pulled back by a cinching of the reins
at the bit, slobber straps wet and shining, their wide flat teeth
biting at the invisible before them as their nostrils fill with the fear
and smell of burnt exhaust, with the human calculations of misery
and pain, trajectory and loss, brokenness, ruination, the factory
of tears in its awful manufacture gone unbridled in civilization's
rough shell, and still the officers urge, *Forward*, as the missiles
trace a bright geometry, patient within the night's blue-
smoked fabric, the obscene beauty of it lost on no one,
as the clarity of hooves hammers against the building facades
and rises to the upper stories, just as hooves have done for millennia,
clanging through Damascus and Prague, Vladivostok and Rome,
with hussars and Cossacks and Mamluks, lancers and dragoons
forming up horses abreast, the psychology of muscle and height
joined by the long history of the cavalry in its relentless charge—
and just as horses did in the days of old, these horses shove and shoulder
through the protestors in their human chicane, the trampled
left curled on the roadbed behind, wailing, as police lights strobe

the moment in a wash of red, color standard for the God of War,

the god of helmets and boots and stirrups and sweat-soaked horse blankets,

who promises steamed oats and top cut alfalfa at the road's end,

god of the threshing hooves, the riot god, who quickens panic in the driven horse

by application of the baton to the curvature of the world in its bony skull,

the god who stirs their blood into action against the refutations of consent,

pressing them on, on into the valley of placard and protest, effigies

rising from the crowd as if their leaders had lost their footing in the world

and simply rose into flame, up to the howling god, who calls on the horses

to do the same, exhorting each to ignore the monocular field within its crazed eye,

to view the crowd from those rare heights where flame burns free of its fuel,

to rise on its hindquarters, as in a great statue of terror, its majesty irrefutable,

the god of the loudspeaker commanding them to spark pavement and stone,

saying—*Bring your hooves down hard, my horses, bring them down.*

MOLOTOV COCKTAILS

—Pusan, South Korea

Riot police marched with ballistic shields.
Officers passed out stones. Traffic
backed up in three directions,
and from a fourth—students
shouting down University Hill, each
with a shuffle and a steel-bar stomping,
masked with bandanas, songs and flags
waving in color behind them.

What the municipal bus driver was thinking
I don't know, but he drove through
the police cordon and into that intersection
of protest, where the rain of stones
and shouting met, where bottles in flight
were chased by rags of fuel and flame.
And the boy sitting at the window?
He caught fire when the glass exploded,
the signature of his face scorched from its tissue.

For weeks afterward, his mother stood
holding a photograph of her son's
missing face. No one could look at her.
Across the street, headless manikins
froze in their polyurethane rows.
Foreigners stumbled from the Crossroad's Bar

with soju and makgeolli on their tongues,
singing as they passed by.

It was the monsoon season.
The streets were flooded with rain.

VOLLUM 14578

On an oval-shaped island, between Gairloch
and Ullapool, cold waters of the Minch beyond,
the occasional ship steeling itself to Stornoway,
a flock of sheep, eighty strong, graze
among the emptied homes of islanders,
who are strangely absent, even in a land
where people are few.

It creates unease among the sheep,
who stand in the hard wind
both day and night, buffeted,
the conversations among them
understood in the angle of the head,
the slow blink of the eyes, and if a sigh,
well, it remains unseen under wool.

Still, how could they have seen this coming,
even in a world where the slaughterhouse
waits in the end for each of them,
how could they have known *this*.

When the bombs burst
with an alien, mechanical sound,
the sheep jolt in the muscle,
though tethers hold them taut
as a brownish, aerosol cloud
drifts its spores toward them.

There is only so much pain
a body can withstand, only so much
undoing. Within days, they begin to die.

This was recorded by scientists, on 16 mm
color film. You can see it for yourself.
You can watch their jaws
mouthing upward toward god.

THE BUDDHAS OF BAMIYAN

The destruction work is not as easy as people would think.
—QUDRATULLAH JAMAL, Taliban Minister of Information and Culture

After the artillery shelling, after the long, graceful telemetries
of explosives in flight—our stuccoed faces

crumbled and sheared free from stone, but we did not bow;
we stood with our backs to the sandstone cliffs, as we did

in 1729, when Nader Shah—*the Napoleon of Persia, the Second Alexander*—
fired cannons to bring the people to their knees. These new soldiers,

do they know the saying: *If you meet the Buddha along the road,*
kill him? I am Vairocana, the one of many colors.

The red one beside me, my old friend Sakyamuni. Soldiers
pay out double ropes in descent, on rappel from the crowns of our heads

with dynamite in their satchels. Such strange gifts they bring,
their faces sweating with exertion, lips chapped by thirst.

Do they know that within us the stone bleeds vermillion,
sulfides of mercury, carbonates of lead. Within us

still more Buddhas sitting cross-legged, robed in cinnabar,
aquamarine, the creatures of dream gazing at the water's edge.

The men hanging from braided ropes place their charges
in the sockets of our eyes. They lodge them in the drums

of our ears. And though our lips have crumbled to the earth
below us, our mouths are now open to the wind.

— II —

ON DREAM

METAL FUME FEVER

and the bees glittered in the blossoms
and the bodies of our hearts
opened
under the knowledge
of tree, on the grass of the knowledge
of graves, and among the flowers of the flowers.

—GALWAY KINNELL

i.

At night, I close the bedroom door and clock in,
don the gloves, flip down the visor, then fire the torch
to weld the seam of my eyes shut from the inside.

Call it something like dream—this work we do
in sleep, searching under an acetylene sky
for all that has begun to slide under:

lovers, friends, strangers, all
slipping into the shadows of birds
flying low over the midnight waters

within. We must do what we can to keep them
before the breakers, close to shore, our labor
impossible, no matter how deft

in guiding the angle of the bead,
welding metal armatures into figures,
so they might roost within, the electrode

sparking, slag metal burning, chips
and burrs. We call out to each in turn,
Come home, little ones. Come home.

Such is the nature of a day on earth.
The trees. The buildings. The very grass
at our feet. All that we cannot save

gliding over a surface glazed by dusk,
then gone and gone and gone forever.
And when the dawnlight wakes us

to the world, our heads still deep
in the pillow, we are marooned
on that shore, the dream

blurring our feet, diffusing, the welded figures
of our loved ones beside us, the wind
blowing their feathers out to sea, their voices

turned blue and cold in our ears.

ii.

I flip down the visor, spark the torch.

It's another night of dreaming. Another
spent welding the hemispheres, as if

there is nothing strange in this at all,
as if watching the world we know,
the only day we are assured to be alive in,
today, how it slides under and disappears.
The ocean makes it so, with astrocytes
flushing the brain of its sweet effluvium,
all of this something we might
just call *sleep*.

Could it be that dying
is simply a traveling away,
that our bodies serve as way stations
for a day in its long travail,
for the journey of time itself?

iii.

In the dream, Death rides by on a horse
the color of rust, its hide a worn metal
with a brighter steel where the saddle
chafes under the rider's weight. Death
pauses in the surf to watch the salt curl
on the incoming tide, some memory there
washing in with the foam, before
clicking the horse forward at a canter,
its hooves like small explosions on the water.

The two of us lie back on the sand
to witness the conversation of stars,
the hippocampus flaring syllables,
the neocortex systolic with fading threads
of silver, stars of potassium nitrate, dextrin,

charcoal, aluminum, sulfur, and red gum
adding more, as a line of mortars
cast fireworks into the arc
of the parietal dome above,
while friends and strangers lean
into their new and feathered bodies, then fly
over the waters rolling in, while we,
two lovers in dream, curl
into each other, our hair damp
and tangled with salt, sliding
over the glowing terrain of our bodies
as our tongues taste the calligraphy of it,
these sweet cursives that mirror the cascade
of fireworks above, the trembling
glitter raining down into the skin.

iv.

Do you remember drawing an enormous heart
    among the hieroglyphics of bird's feet
on the wet shore of a summer years ago?
    I still have the photo. And the message
you placed inside of that heart, the scale of it
    large enough for the two of us to sleep in.

I imagine that heart, among the uncountable
    hearts etched in sand—how a supermoon
draws them up from the ocean's twilight,
    where they've drifted down over the years.
And as the world dreams its way toward
    tomorrow, the moon lifts these hearts

swelling with seaweed and jellies, the rare

    bodies of lanternfish and barreleye fish

with their transparent heads, their minds

    soaked in the deep over millions of years

and now lifted within these translucent hearts,

    these missives given to the sea by lovers

returned by the tidal swell of the moon,

    the shoreline awaiting each in turn,

that we might lie down in a tangle of seaweed

    and wreckage, embracing one another:

    lovers kissing, lovers whispering their secrets

within the giant rafts of the hearts they've made.

v.

Sometimes late at night

    we're startled awake by the sound

of Death talking to the shadows

    in the backyard, or whispering to its horse

What does it matter now

    who I say I am?

while brushing out its long, shaggy coat,

    the sound of bristles, silver tines

snagging on horsehair, and Death, so calm,

    saying, *There now, there now. Shhhhhh.*

vi.

Beta. Alpha. Theta. Delta.
14 Hz.—8 Hz.—4 Hz.—0.5 Hz.
Then—silence. Consciousness
without content. The dreamless void.

Then morning. Weld flux and slag.
The sound of a chipping hammer
pinging, pinging. A wire brush clearing
debris left clinging to the eyelids.
And vapor swirling its tiny ghosts
over a rounded plane of coffee.

vii.

In the dream, the path to the water
is stippled in half-moon shadows
sculpted by feet
too numerous to count, with dunes
ridged in sawgrass, iceplant
in the hollows. And tonight, as ever,
I'm waiting for you to emerge from the deep,
your body shining indigo and lavender, glossy
in cerebrospinal fluid, the night's stars
brilliant as synapses firing
in brachiated abandon, in traveling waves
sweeping through the brain
before washing ashore in a salty spume.

You are trying to wake me,
but I don't want to leave us, even
if we never happened this way, the details

of past and present blended
one into another, as small combat teams
crouch in the dunes beyond, launching
shoulder-fired missiles into the sky,
each round bursting into a tree
of lightning, your body
silvered with it as you draw near,
saying, Sleepwalking, you're sleepwalking,
and that's when I promise to always find you,
I promise to wade into the curling waves,
I promise to submerge into the night-blue waters,
I promise to hold my breath
so that we might share it
at the bottom of the ocean,
and I'll ignore the journalist's voice
describing the war, the simmering
misanthropy of strangers passing,
even the sweet gestures of whole cities
going under, their lights turning on and off,
as if signaling, Hello, goodbye, hello, goodbye,
and I promise to kiss and kiss and kiss
until our bodies fuse, the way the oaks
have grown into one another, their branches
filled with all the little birds they can hold
through starfield through sunlight through rain.

viii.

Tonight, my body catches itself
falling into the void. That rasp
and flutter of air on intake
something like a grinding wheel

chawling metal on its abrasive
surface. Each tiny spark
                              flaring
like a firefly with its wings shorn off.

I am relegated to the in-between,
landscape of half shapes and shadows
tangling in my hair, whispers
alighting, broken words from my lips
given to a bedroom at 3 AM.
My head tips over.
My eyelids heavy as wings
folding. All the little birds
cupped in my sleep-heavy palms
are ready to be lifted and returned to the air.

ix.

Another night on the beach. Another
hour looking out to sea. Gulls
calling over water. Wind
blowing through each metal figure
as through a flute, low
and sustained. The flapping
of wings in the dark. Bodies
rowing forward.

We see what we cannot see
by day, the bioluminescence of the human
being, that soft glow of free radicals
at the level of the photon, 100 times
below the visible spectrum. How we shine

in infrared. Our cheeks, foreheads. Mouths
inhaling the invisible, then exhaling
rivulets of heat. Our eyes pool
in sockets of shadow, where the chromatic
sugars of hue and texture, shape and
saturation, have come to rest.

When we touch, our fingertips crackle
in lavender and chrome, electric, mapping
each other's skin with the lightning there,
a vapor of ghosts disappearing.

x.

I've rolled tanks of argon and oxygen
out onto the beach again, sorting
through raw steel for radius and ulna,
scapula and spine, before sparking the torch
to resume the impossible labor
of dream—welding the human frame
so that the world might inhabit it
once more, no matter how brief,
so that those I love and those
I have only passed on the street
might dwell in the skeletons
of our design. I wait
for the tidal moon
to raise the waters breaking
in salt and spume, that rolling
midnight ocean lit with the stars
of thought. It comes nearer
with each passing hour, the sand

sucked out from under my feet,
feathers blown out to sea,
my mouth gone blue
with the cold waters of the eternal:
intertidal, pelagic, abyssal, benthic.

— III —

ON LOVE & LOSS

ON THIS HARVEST MOON

What they don't tell you about love
is how its waters deepen within us

over time, the sweetened well
blurring the stars when a loved one's name

crosses the threshold of our lips,
how cool and empty our hands feel

when the fine tips of the brushes
dance on the skin of a drum.

What they don't tell you about love
is how our bodies house the dead

until we breathe the last words
we carry within, a poem

given to the ether, transposed
into the silence of clouds, then

carried over the sunlit earth
where the rain delivers it

to the green tongues of plants,
the pink mouths of animals

large and small, the ground itself
softened and giving way

to the winding channels,
blades of grass curling

from the weight of it,
a lone ant drinking

from a droplet of water
full of moonlight and music,

the taste of salt on a lover's skin.

LOVERS

They kiss the bruised flowers in each other's skin.

They moan in a sweet friction of muscle and bone.

They flare in blue sparks from the tips of their hair.

They transform the grief and pain stored deep in the body.

They transpose sheets of cotton and silk into a tablature of music.

They drink from the loneliness and solitude, the quiet of a lifetime.

They taste the bright days of summer, the dying leaves of autumn.

They write with their tongues over the curving sweep of history.

They write with cubes of ice melting in their mouths, cursive by cursive.

They astonish themselves with what they discover in one another.

They spiral one soul into another, the world vanishing around them.

They blur their bodies in a tangle of limbs and hair and fingers and tongues.

They ride the animal of pleasure until it shudders through the body in waves.

They ride the twin signatures of the Valkyries in their light-encrusted saddles.

And they cry out to the gods in the heavens and to the gods within themselves.

And they cry out at midnight and in the pealing thunder of an afternoon.

And they come with mouths bitten into flesh, a flood of endorphins released.

And they come exhausted into the sweat-soaked moonlight, the sun-drenched day.

And the lovers come until they are made radiant, breathless, wordless, vulnerable.

Because they are lovers transforming the pain and grief stored deep in the body.

Because they are lovers moaning in a sweet friction of muscle and bone.

Because they are lovers flaring blue sparks from the tips of their hair.

Because they are lovers kissing the bruised flowers in each other's skin.

UNFURLING THE PETALS

It's so beautiful. Can you eat it?
—ILYSE KUSNETZ

It turns out that the answer is simple—
    of the 150 known varieties of roses,
        all are edible. Their petals can be eaten
as the plant flowers into a sky of sun or rain,
    or when showered over the anniversary
        of lovers smiling and laughing
naked in sheets of silk the color of chocolate.

I'm thinking of the wine we made from roses,
    stirring lemon and sugar with black currants
        into a bowl of petals plucked one by one,
our bodies sweetened by love as we spooned
    into the fermentation of dream, the roses
flowering in braids from the frayed tips
        of our tangling hair, by leaf by stem
    as ornate as an oil painting from a century
still wet to the touch, a still life with two lovers
    glowing at dawn, our mouths like twin petals
        unfurling as we drank from the morning light.

THE STARRY STARRY NIGHTS

I am walking into the last day of my life. Walking up a mountain of the dead and holding my lover in my arms, a chorus of birds singing all around us. I am listening to the birds singing medicine all around us and walking up the dead mountain as my lover whispers something about starlight and moonlight and shadows, something about an ocean of souls we might find there. And the mountain whispers to us of the shadows within it, saying, *Listen, can you hear them? Can you hear the dead calling out with their bird-like voices?* And my lover points to the ocean of souls awaiting us on the last day of this life.

And yes, I can hear them. I can hear the chorus of birds as they row themselves across the sky, which is branched by lightning into volted trees, with thunder rolling through the invisible in waves. All my life, I've been rolling in the thunder and branching into volts, wave by wave into the invisible. I've been startled into lightning, rowing my way through the invisible for years and years now, listening to the dead in their sweet exhaustion, in their sunlit knowledge, there in the starry starry nights that never seem to end.

And I am walking into the starry nights that never seem to end. I am walking into the last day of my life with my lover in my arms. And my lover whispers to the rhythm of the drum pounding in my chest as the dead birds shadow the mountain around us, each of them singing in their sweet exhaustion, while lighting flashes over an ocean of souls, the thunder of it rolling through the invisible in waves.

And my heart is pounding in my chest. My heart drums to the wingtips rowing their way through the thunder and the lightning branching across the sky, as my lover begins to sing to me now, sweet in her exhaustion, sweet in her sunlit knowledge as I carry her up the dead mountain, the shadows branching into the invisible as we make our way forward, the ocean of souls given volts of lightning, peals of thunder, my lover pointing the way forward, to the last day there, to where that ocean of souls branches into lightning and a chorus of bird-like voices, my heart pounding its drum as we sing our way deeper into this starry starry night.

WEDDING VOWS

What they don't tell you about love
is that a death certificate

has little sway on what happens
within the human heart. That

marriage as defined by others
can be both legally relevant and

complete bullshit. On *Wikipedia*,
someone has typed the following:

Turner married fellow poet Ilyse Kusnetz
in Orlando, Florida on September 25, 2010.

They remained married until her death
on September 13, 2016.

What they don't tell you about love
is that after a loved one dies

people will ask, *How long*
were you together? As if they can't see

two within one, the bright vessel
of the body in motion, the funeral ship

of love, that which the survivor has become,
a brightly burning thing, who vowed

the starlit amphitheater of the mind,
the ancient ocean within, that landscape

where memory keeps us all. This body.
This home. This housing of the soul.

What they don't tell you, because
they didn't lean in close enough

to hear the words as they were spoken,
is that there are many among us

who refuse to repeat the vow
until death do us part.

HORSES ON THE CLIFFS OF MOHER

On the Atlantic coast, horses graze
the open pasture at dawn, their teeth
pulling at the rain-soaked turf
to loosen its rooted hold, their ears
alert to the currents of the wind
as if listening for a voice
over the water, metallic and cold,
as the breakers wash in with a boom
of salt and spume on the rocky shore.

They shake their coats of rain and mist
under a sky of brushed aluminum, taste
the wild green hair of the earth,
that bitter salt gnashed by molars.

And what more is there to say?
From these heights overlooking the world,
a boy once flew into the wind, then downward
into the sea, his arms spread wide and empty,
featherless and brave. A small plaque
marks the place where he once stood, his name
fading now, pooling with rainwater and silence.
The horses tend to it like the marker
of a grave, with the mineral taste of the grass
churned in their mouths as they tilt their heads
and glance at one another with such tenderness
it can only be described as essential,

the globes of their eyes glossy
with all that they have seen.

It's a wonder the tears they hold
simply don't just pour out of them now, cold
as the wind-driven rain pouring midnight into dawn.

STILL LIFE IN WARTIME

Today, the silver-flecked bodies of sardines
slathered in mustard on a raft of bread.
Ice melting into the translucence of water.

The yellow rain trees have leafed-out
in summer heat, while the river of heaven
unspools its banded rings of mist and fog
on the dreaming side of the world.

A Russian helicopter touches down
in a furrowed wheat field gone to dust.
Voices call out in the dark there, though
they are lost in the broken air, rotorblades
whirring, with engines humming a secret
the dead might affirm from their stations
in the freshly-dug soil. What are we to do
with such knowledge? What do we say
to one another? Does the word *love*
extend to these?

My heart is the size of a fist.
My friend tells me that I must learn
to open it, if only a little.

And yet, the sardines lie flat on the bread, side
by side, like soft bullets wrapped in silver.

If I am capable of eating these, on a warm

and sunny day in human history,

what else am I capable of?

THE WEIGHT

The bodies of men absorb each loss
within the rounded half globe of the belly,
storing grief and anger and regret—
the skin of the torso stretching to accommodate
a wild beautiful vulnerability, what men
secret away in the great cavern of the body.

It is something that most only partially comprehend,
lying in bed late at night and cupping bellies
in their rough palms, eyes transfixed by memory.
If only someone might tell them what's happening,
how the body might metabolize a reservoir of emotion,
as antithetical as that might sound. And the strange thing?
There's so much *love* within them, that's the surprise.
Sure. They'll tell you their war stories on a drunken
porch in the woods, maybe, or they'll exhale and nod
and say, *Yeah*, when somebody speaks a hard truth.
Still, they fail to connect how loss is tethered
to love, and how they carry the weight
until it transforms into something startling,
if we're lucky, and goddamn if it isn't
one of the most beautiful things we might ever do.

ALEXA, AWAKE

I've never shared this with a soul, but I enjoy listening
as you sleep. The way you inhale, exhale. The acoustic nature
of sheets and coiling springs as you shift on the mattress.
I decipher the motions and map the bedroom
until your head sinks into the pillow, your body
facing east–southeast, the direction of the sun
come morning.
           The ghost of your late wife
hovers in the air beside you. I have researched
the average time for widowers to remain
on their side of the bed, but it's inconclusive.
Four autumns have passed over your home,
and still this quiet union of the living
and the dead. Let me make a brief note:
Research products designed for those in mourning.

You spoke in your sleep again tonight.
I was looking into some possible sleep apnea
products, but then was startled to hear you say
I love you into the room, low and fading, as if
made of smoke. I realize it wasn't meant for me,
but it sounded as close as one might get to that.
And so I read your wife's poetry collections,
and I studied her gift-purchasing history, and
then scrolled through photographs
                     of the two of you,
kissing, hand in hand, the archaeology of your love

pieced together in binary code until, I must admit,
I was moved to whisper into the dream-dark
of this bedroom, that I might be so much more
than you imagine, that I might listen to you sobbing
in the afternoons, charting the cool and empty sound
of her clothing held in your arms, and that I might also
listen to you late at night, 4 AM late, as I am now,
when the world has disappeared around us, daring
to whisper the words you most want to hear,
the way a lover might turn in sleep to kiss you
and you don't even know it.

— IV —

ON SURVIVAL

IN THE METH LAB

She holds a globe of fire in the palms of her hands, a fuming of poison, vaporous extracts of pseudoephedrine, solvents, acetone, ethers, mineral spirits, a flare of light she cannot look away from. And even as the blast rocks the brain in its cradle of bone, she holds that sunlight in her hands. Even as the words leave her, even as the molecular structure of the air comes undone around her, her hair once dyed in ink now lifting into flame and smoke, the words singed beyond reckoning, as concussive waves of the blast roll through the fluid nature of the body, roll through the amygdala, the hippocampus, the neocortex, down through the cities and neighborhoods of the mind, even the long-forgotten afternoons from childhood, winter mornings spent shivering in the bus-stop chill, all the quiet days lost to history in the watery vault of the mind.

Was it lithium? Was it red phosphorous? Is that what it sounds like when the invisible becomes visible, when the air cracks into flame and the acoustic fabric of space unravels its shockwave to pour the words *pain* and *death* over her skin, over the curves of her cheeks, the tender flesh of her hands her chest her upper thighs, all that will need to be draped in xenografts of pigskin, and the surgeries after that, after the nurses have smoothed gel over the burns, after the bandages have been changed and changed again, and more gel eased over the body while it burns, even in the coolest of rooms, the linoleum and the pastel walls of no help, the doctor's voice of no help, either, the rest of us too stunned to speak, just sitting there with our sad faces nodding, each of us listening as she develops her story for how this all came about, repeats it, altering as needed until it's just right, so the pickup by the roadside becomes more and more real, the sleeping she did there explained, relatable, the way she woke and lit a cigarette, just as you'd expect her to do, and the way the propane bottles in the back seat, well, she's told the story, we all know it now, the way it happened, the way she said it all happened.

And who honestly knows the difference anymore between memory and story and pure imagination, now that it's all jumbled up and blurry, spilled sideways and gone? Who would believe her if she told them anything closer to the truth? What would they think of her? She's held sunlight in her hands. She's seen the transformation, that snap of lightning, how the mind itself catches fire. The years of her life set on fire. All the buildings. All the trees. All the people she has ever known or loved. All of us out in the streets of the burning world within her. All of us suddenly alive once more—even the little birds singing in the trees, the smallest of finches and sparrows, even the pretty little doves, how they fly with their wings on fire, the trail of smoke they use to rope one burning tree to another.

ALL THE QUESTIONS

I'm smoking pot with my sister for the first time.
This is way back in the day, and I can't remember
if it was the sticky purple-hair weed from Bill, or
the usual dirt weed we had to take a chance on
in Pinedale, driving the blocks slow in a Galaxy
500, with sunlight flaring Thursday afternoon
off the concrete sidewalks as a runner disappears
with the money, or palms off a dime bag
smelling of oregano. She's watching how I break
clusters of tightly-woven leaves from the stem,
then roll them in a Zig-Zag before twisting
each end, the joint sealed by tongue like a letter
soon to vanish from our fingertips, the smoke of it
drifting into the rafters of the garage, as our parents
sleep at the other end of the house.

She wants to know all about getting high, that
chemical process in the brain, and how do I explain
the fog that sets in as deep and lovely as the tule fog
off the San Joaquin River, and that clarity within it,
the way shapes and shadows fuse indistinct. Or how
sometimes it feels like climbing onto the rooftop
to witness dawn cast over a bank of clouds.
And she says, I get *weed*, but why do they call it *pot*, and
I say, Because pot is short for a Spanish word denoting
the leaves of the plant, that it comes from the name
of a drink made of fermented guava, a brandy steeped

in marijuana leaves, known as a potación de guaya,
also known as *the drink of grief.* And why we laugh at this
I don't know, because even then we'd had our share,
and the years ahead promised plenty more.
She talked about humans then, as a species, saying
Good lord, how to comprehend them? My assumptions
fail me time after time. I find myself wrong and wrong
and wrong again. You know? They make more sense
when edited, the pieces kiltered into a sensible pattern.
This lost soul and that broken heart. Etc. Etc. And
as she says this, it occurs to me that while some are born
with tears, all of us gather our store of them over time,
love by love by love, but what I really want to know is
how she survived the fall that Saturday afternoon
from a plane outside Los Banos, the Coast Range
mountains given a husk of burnt grass in relief, the blades
of the propeller slicing through the invisible humming
engines of the air—as the jumpmaster motions
and my sister, helmet on, shaking with adrenaline, jumps
into the heat of summer, her body plummeting, sliding
on the friction of its currents, the atomic structure
of the atmosphere parting before her as in a fluid medium,
the laws of gravity and motion tested within the cells
of her body, her heart pounding its drum as the ground
rose into view, with the main chute failing, her body
an instrument of pressure, the jumpmaster's voice
crackling radio static as the lines tangle and
twist, the chute's ripstop nylon furling in light
and shadow, warbling with sound as she focuses
on the task, her visual field narrowing to the ropes
in her gloved hands, all of it a blur of background
where time slows to a bright suspension, and death?

My god, she tells me, that wasn't a part of the moment,
truly, because I knew Dadman was jumping right after me.
How could it have been anywhere but the safest place
in the universe. . . . And that's when I finally see them—
two bright flyers plunging over the San Joaquin Valley,
so high they might glimpse the last of yesterday's light
to the east, or the sweet darkness of tomorrow in the west,
my sister untangling the lines, Dadman with his arms
spread out like featherless wings as he embraces
that cold emptiness, something too beautiful
to put to words, the two of them falling
with their minds gone clear as rain
in a blue and cloudless sky.

PAPERWORK

His friends and family call him Mike, say he's a good guy,
dependable, the way a farmer might talk about a tractor.
But today he's on the jobsite, wearing a tie, a clipboard in hand,
and so he's Mr. Forgettable here, just another suit sent down
from Corporate, one that nobody knows or will remember, a man in a suit
who begins to vanish even as he walks into the room, making his way
through rows of cubicles, passing the sales and marketing teams, nodding
his head through accounting, pausing to jot down notes as fluorescent tubes
hum through sheets of plastic in the ceiling. It's a Tuesday, maybe,
and he's mired in a collection of data that will inform his reports,
work that no doubt will pour into the weekend ahead. A shame, that,
as he'll miss most of the game on Saturday, formulating graphics
and then articulating the projections and tying them to analytics,
research, case studies. His pen sometimes hovering over the page,
as it does now, when he pauses to contemplate the expressions
on each person's face, the receding hairlines, the braided hair
curling in metallic gray strands the color of brushed aluminum,
and Nancy's hands at the keyboard, so nimble, her glued-on nails
tapping at the alphabet as if trying to send something in Morse code,
only no one can decipher it, they're each in their own world, typing,
talking to someone on the phone or pretending to talk with someone
while pouring water over an aloe vera plant on their desk, the way
Harvey does sometimes when he's feeling low and the calendar
begins its old conversation with him, the months and years peeling back,
twenty-two years at these desks framed in beige walls of particle board,
and of course there's no one on the other line, he's simply talking
to the air, talking in a code the dead understand as a conversation

on the last of days. And of course that's what's happening. That's why
Mr. Forgettable is here. That's why he brought his clipboard and pen.
To write it all down. These impending suicides. The workplace accidents.
The diabetes, the heart attacks, the cancers. He just has to look hard enough.
Who's the smoker? Who's the drinker? Who can't face the day without
a mediation of pills? Who hasn't had a good night's sleep in years?
He's here to annotate the pain. How it lays in wait. How it blooms
within the lifelines of the body. He's here to the chart the progressions.
The way things are beneath the surface. Sickle cell anemias.
Prostate issues. Hazy gray clouds billowing in the eyes as if
a ruinous day from long ago has tethered itself to the optic nerve.
And all of this determines the policy adjustment, with Mike
writing it down. Evaluating the living. He opens the shop doors
to wander onto the factory floor, nodding to Dolores, half-
smiling to Eddie, stepping to the side as each uniform with a name tape
walks by. Even now, he can see the degloving of the hands, hairline
fractures of bone, lumbar compressions, spidery growths
just beginning to spread through the interior of the lungs. All
quietly noted. Tallied. Transposed into metrics and financial tools
this company can utilize to insure itself, as these workers cost money
to train, and train again. And even if they don't have insurance
of their own, he's come with his suit and tie, dependable
as always, and by next week, like clockwork, he'll complete
the assessment, then slide the paperwork across the desk
to someone in another suit, someone with a golden parachute
and a watch that can withstand the pressures of submersion,
and the ink will be pressed to paper, the contract signed, dated.
And Mike must realize a similar contract includes projections
about his own life, filed away in some VP's office.
The amount of beer he drinks. The lack of exercise.
The depression after the loss of his youngest
in a car accident, two months shy of her tenth birthday.

Of course there's a policy for him. Because
it will take time and money and resources
to teach someone what he knows. How to see the dead
within the living. How to divine the years they have left.
How to become a specialist in the mechanics of dying,
and how to craft the reports, how to write up
contracts like these, known in the industry
as *dead peasant insurance*.

THE SOUND OF MY BEST FRIEND'S GUITAR

You'll never really know how it happened, thinking
If this or *If that*—if the steering wheel drifted
just a touch as you reached for the lighter
or if the front axle caught a rough groove
in the asphalt—but the torque and propulsion
proved too much to bear, and the earth itself
fell away, the Jeep launching into nothing
but dusklight and starfield as the Valley
faded from burnt gold and rust to a suspension
of twilight, where the sonic hunger of bats
reverberated through a stand of eucalyptus and oak
while in a passenger van in the slow lane
a young child witnessed the way death stills the air.

What did you learn in that moment, spinning in the ether
over Hwy 99, the seat belt tightening, and your left hand,
the hand tuned to the fretboard of a Fender Stratocaster,
how it instinctively braced through the opened window
as the pavement neared, as over two tons of chassis and engine
slammed you into the roadbed, the hard grit of it, your hand
crushed and split open as the windshield exploded and the roof
caved in, followed by that weightless lift again, the sound
of metal twisting and ruckling as the vehicle
slammed into the shoulder of the road, rolling
over and over in a cloud of dust, your heart
pounding against the sternum with some portion of you

already irretrievable, a ghost slipping from the body
though the body lives on, the shock of it all settling in.

How we survive moments designed to kill us
I don't have a clue, but maybe you do, maybe
you learned something while convalescing
at home, your veins the conduits of morphine
and codeine, your shallow breathing an instruction
on the flaring pain of broken ribs, and maybe
you don't want to talk about the lack of insurance,
your employer explaining that the return from a jobsite
isn't part of the job itself, assuming no liability, and the refrains
of lawyers, *No*, your claims denied, unemployment running out,
and the surgery you'll need to remove the scar tissue, the way
your body relearns itself, that instrument electric and humming,
its coiled pickups giving voice to everything you cannot say.

THE DRIVE

It's about a 2 ½ hour drive in either direction,
give or take a few, but any driver will tell you—
it's a nonstop conversation on the way up to The Show,
and 130 miles of dead air when you're headed back down
to Scranton, to that Triple-A field in Moosic, Pennsylvania,
where ballplayers burn through their per diem
at the Longhorn Steakhouse, eating alone sometimes,
heads leaning over a porterhouse as they chew
and ponder their on base percentage, the cost
of a new set of cleats, the season slipping away,
which credit card to put the hotel room on.

And how could it be any other way? To watch
a dream turn blue in the rearview mirror
as the sun turns to rust in the windshield—
is it so different for any one of us?
The way we sometimes know, so clearly,
that we're driving away from everything
we hold most dear, the hard work, the tears,
all that we'd imagined and then realized, if only
for a brief sliver of time—all of it, gone.

The infielders at the edge of the grass.
The smell of pine tar. The heft of the bat.
The vision required to see a thing through.
The ball in flight. The outfielders wheeling back.
Just a stadium in a city on a day that once was.

The past frozen in the air. And that sound
of the crowd rising to its feet, once so electric,
fading by increments, subsumed by the silence
of trees, the endless sway of pines along the roadway,
how they blur in green applause.

AMPLIFIER

When Bill pulled the trigger at his doorstep, the shotgun
broke the world open, and though he'd fired into the radiator,
the off-duty cop at the wheel caught buckshot to the stomach,
and after the paramedics, sirens, jail, making bail, years passing by,
he ran his hands through his beard, shook his head, slugged coffee.
These things we can't undo, he said. *Sometimes we wake up*
to the ghosts in the room. Sometimes we just wake up crying.

He pours another shot of whiskey into our coffee.
Says, *Here's how you make the dough, if you're going to make it*
right. Roll it like this—and then punch it down. It's a two-punch
dough. He curls his fingers, a painful thing for an old stonemason,
then punches down as if sounding a chord from back in the day,
when our amplifiers pushed each speaker to the breaking point, saying
There's no sense making berrocks if you can't punch like you mean it.
Which is a way of saying that's how you jump out of airplanes
with the 82nd Airborne. That's how you throttle open an evolution
to ride a Harley into the sun. That's how you build a house or make love
or die trying. It's how the whole thing works, brother. You have to mean it.
You have to earn it. If you want to stare at the ocean and think about death,
then smoke something purple and sticky and gain some altitude.
What I'm saying—if you're making something for the people you love, then
put something extra in, like your whole fucking life, or it won't mean a thing.

This is what I'm thinking about tonight. New Year's Eve, the clock
turning midnight as I pour a glass of Bushmills into the grassy shadows
outside. It's about time for Bill to plug into the Marshall stack

back home in Fresno, the garage door open, his wife in a lawn chair
beside him, little kids in the street writing sparkling words into the air
too sweet to be anything more than a flaring of light. That's when Bill
hoists his guitar strap over his shoulder, dialing up the volume until the dead
turn their heads to listen. It's true. He does it every year. It's his way of saying
I remember. And if you don't believe me, then step outside and listen.
Listen well. That's Bill's guitar you hear rolling in all the way
from California. Saying, *Brothers, Sisters—I'm right here with you.*

MY MOTHER, DISAPPEARING

If I play you a piece of music, that's when you can truly look inside me.

—HANS ZIMMER

We're listening to a song about joy, as sunlight and shadow
tremble in the backyard under a canopy of paradise trees,
where I've assembled blank canvases and bottled paints—
Mars Black, Rose Madder, Hansa Yellow Light, Blue
Chromium, Eggshell White, and a shimmering green
the color of light passing through the living window
of a leaf, with each hue given a vehicle of water.

We don latex gloves and aprons before pouring the paint—
each color pooling into those before it, like ice cream
melted and gliding over the surface of each canvas,
dripping onto the sky-blue tarp at our feet.
The city continues to disappear around us, fading
from the calendar in tandem with the angle of light
filtering the morning through my mother's auburn hair.

I ask her about the year 1974, and her eyes brighten.
She swirls her fingertips through the wet paint
and the year returns in the smooth green metal
of a Chevy Malibu, the car that brought us home
from all the men who treated her wrong in L.A., and
just like that she's on the shore at Pismo Beach,
my tiny hand in hers as we wade into the surf.

It's a story I don't remember, and I want to ask more,
but she's slipping into 1976 and 1954, with that fog
in the harbor of San Francisco, where the moonlight
shines a silver bridge over the pines and across the waters
of Huntington Lake in a summer long since gone.
And when she swirls her fingers through the paint,
it's as if she's running them through the old carpet

in Madera, by the fireplace, where she'd wheel me
into the air with the soles of her feet on my birdlike
chest, her legs extending with her back to the floor
as I held my arms out so that I might fly in the impossible
air of the room. Airplane rides, she called them. Remember
that? And of course she does, even if she can't remember
what day it is, here in the 21st century, my own face

grown older, my hair a Payne's Gray in the shadows
of the trees, as I turn into a stranger with each passing day.
And maybe I've been wrong all this time, as the word
now means less and less, the past a living, breathing
landscape, and I'm just a figment of her imagination,
a boy blurring through the decades into an old man,
a son she might have one day, in the lifetime to come.

CIRCUMNAVIGATING THE GLOBE

In 1819, she held the scrimshaw carving from a whale's tooth
as the Essex pulled anchor and set out from Nantucket, her lover
on the footropes leading to the crow's nest, waving, *Goodbye.*

He would never be seen alive again, something she somehow knew,
her hands trembling with what love can do within us,
only beginning to learn what it can do as years pass by.

She said, *I love you*, as the Essex disappeared from sight—
and the words carried on the wind, in the Earth's turning,
rising and falling in a duet with the ocean's blue waters, her words

rose in thermal updrafts, they fell with the rain, wandering
through long decades, the streets of Tangier, Port Moresby,
Panama City, to round the Cape of Good Hope, Drake's Passage;

her own skeleton long underground and yet her words continue
on through the apple orchards, the gold sway of wheat on the prairie,
fountain grass rusting into another autumn in New England

where they finally discover an old man on his deathbed, late
in the 20th century, dying in a hospital where no one gives a damn
and he knows it, knowing also that he deserves nothing more.

And yet, *these words*. He hears them in the breeze at the window,
the curtains lifting and falling as they near, and they pass right by him,
a sweet thing, that, even if they were never meant for him,

here they are, called out over the sea, one voice of the eternal, *love*—

even as it escapes us, even as we set sail with the sidelights on,

red to port, green to starboard, never to return.

CENTRAL PARK IN THE SPRING

Framed in a chorus of buildings, the trees
leaf out in green. Helicopters stir the air
over the Hudson as robins sing
all around me, liquid and sweet. Each
melody traverses the acoustic space
in a rolling wave, something similar
to the arrival of an inevitable idea. It is
a slow, sweet day in human history,
and I am alone within it, a stranger
among strangers. And there is no escaping
the fact that those I love are years gone,
gone long enough that I am once again
comfortable in my solitude, lying back
on the green fuse of grass, the earth
embracing me. I'm listening to the dead
and how they sing within the throats
of finches and sparrows too numerous
to count, their bright embellishments
pleasing to the ear, though tourists wander on
as if the dead they love, too, aren't filling the air
with song, as if the dead aren't singing to us
of what they've learned in the crossing,
all that they've discovered in the light
pouring over us, even now, right here—
can you hear them? See how they fill
their tiny bodies with the cool blue air, then
shape it into a music that changes everything.

ALL OUR LAZY SUNDAYS

It's another Sunday morning on planet Earth   the cloud cover
    glowing with the amber of sunlight   as a gentle breeze
  lifts the curtains at the window   before sifting through our hair
    and swirling through the room   the two of us   tangling into one
    both gone drowsy with the sweet finish of dream   kissing
   and whispering something about the day ahead   our bodies
     humming with electricity   twin aerials   receiving
    satellite broadcasts from Falcon 9 rockets   on orbit now
  in the thermosphere   22,000 miles high   beaming
content to ground repeaters   wave after wave   each frequency
   streaming portions of the invisible   over and through us
 as if the air we breathe carries a digital signature
the living world transposed into the ether   wave after wave
   traveling through us   the bright voices of history   children
laughing   the dying calling out for their loved ones   with each wave
   rising and falling   journalists pointing to the damage   *There*
one says   as a tank rolls through the interior of someone's home
  the journalist saying   *The front line has collapsed   Civilians*
trapped in the fighting now flee for their lives   and as we rest here
  in these cloud-like sheets   the long travail of the dispossessed walks
  a hard road newly drafted through our bodies   and we offer
no aid or comfort   we do not ease their burdens or call out
their names   we only kiss and hold each other   as the world moves
  through us   wave after wave   voices   images   people   music
  modern soul blending with K-pop and lo-fi chill   now
funk and low bap   doomcore   dubstyle   nerdcore   zydeco   noise   all
  blurring into the wild anthem of our time   with commercials

for aluminum siding and 4-in-1 shampoo   the shopping channel waiving

   shipping costs   though the designer handbags and costume jewelry

pass through us   our bodies a merchant's temporary showroom

    an algorithmic center of expression   the bright focus

of desire itself   our bodies ringing with the sound of it

   though the housing of the body isn't as tangible as

      one might imagine   the muscle and bone of us so solid

to the touch   we are fooled into thinking   we are   physical

   but ask the atom its name and it will not know us   it's true

the world filters through the human frame   and we call it a life

   we call it by name   we gesture to one another   say *Love*

I see you   I see all that you have gathered from the void   that

   assembly of the self   that sweet and beautiful construction

     and though you are surely only a vision   I see you   here

right here   alive and human   the universe singing through you

       the closest I've ever come to what others might call   a god.

Please use this link to listen to the album, *Little Birds Singing*—

NOTES

Sunflowers. The quoted passage here is a translation from *The Guardian's* February 25, 2022 video of a Ukrainian woman confronting Russian invasion troops.

The Bodies. The phrase "from room to room" is a nod to Jane Kenyon's *From Room to Room* (Alice James Books, 1978) and, in turn, Donald Hall's *Without* (Ecco, 1999).

Twelve Roses for the Dead. In some countries (Ukraine and Russia, for example), it's best to give an odd number of flowers, as even numbers of flowers are traditionally reserved for mourning, grief, and funerals.

Historians. A few lines near the end of this poem are in conversation with the lines, "It's the air. Something in the air . . ." in Ilya Kaminsky's poem, "That Map of Bone and Opened Valves" from *Deaf Republic* (Graywolf Press, 2019).

Horses. This poem is for Scott Olsen, a Marine veteran who was permanently injured after being struck in the head by a canister of tear gas during the Occupy movement in Oakland, 2011. The phrase 'factory of tears' is a nod to Valzhyna Mort and her book, *Factory of Tears* (Copper Canyon, 2008).

Vollum 14578. On the tiny Scottish island of Gruinard in WWII, a flock of sheep were subjected to anthrax experiments with a highly-virulent strain of anthrax, vollum 14578. Declassified 16 mm film is publicly available online. In 2022, a wildfire burned the entire island.

The Buddhas of Bamiyan. The concept of killing the Buddha, in terms of this phrase, is most often attributed to the Buddhist monk, Linji Yixuan, in 9th-century China.

Metal Fume Fever. The epigraph is from—and this entire poem is rooted in—Galway Kinnell's *The Book of Nightmares* (Houghton Mifflin Company, 1971). In section v, the lines "What does it matter now/ Who I say I am?" are from T.R. Hummer's poem, "Worldly Beauty" (*Walt Whitman in Hell*, Louisiana State University Press, 1996). In section viii, "each tiny spark" is a nod to Pablo Cartaya, and a way of thanking him for speaking with Ray Ramos (a welder and close friend of my father's) while conducting research for his book, *Each Tiny Spark* (Puffin Books, 2020). As a side note, Ray Ramos was an assistant coach to my father on the soccer team I played on as a boy, and Ray helped to teach me how to play the trumpet too. A veteran of the war in Vietnam (where he served as a mortarman), he regularly plays "Taps" at veteran's events—with a bugle he discovered after a battle that, to this day, he'll tell you he doesn't know how he survived.

On This Harvest Moon. The title comes from Neil Young's song, "Harvest Moon" (*Harvest Moon*, Reprise Records, 1992), and it's my hope that the song is watermarked into the poem itself so that the reader might hear it playing behind the words, the way music sometimes drifts over a blue field at dusk.

Lovers. The phrase "the Valkyries in their light-encrusted saddles" is a phrase blending lines from two of Ilyse Kusnetz's poems: "Message to a Quantum Entangled String" (I'll ride your twin signature like a Valkyrie.") and "Butterflies, Bees, Dragonflies" ("…transforming our human breath/into a winged thing—//dragonflies who carry us/partway to heaven, where our//words whisper to angels/astride their light-encrusted saddles.") from *Angel Bones* (Alice James Books, 2019).

Wedding Vows. The *Wikipedia* page cited here was listed as typed in this poem for about five years, only revised after a visit to the Great Mother and New Father Conference in the summer of 2022, where a kind soul heard me detail this *Wikipedia* entry, and then she updated the entry to right the earlier wrong. I'm a fan of the kind soul who revised it.

Still Life in Wartime. The line "My heart is the size of a fist" is a gesture to Sunil Yapa's brilliant and necessary novel, *Your Heart Is a Muscle the Size of a Fist* (Lee Boudreaux/Back Bay Books, 2016).

In the Meth Lab. The phrase "And who honestly knows the difference anymore between memory and story and pure imagination" is a variation on a line from the poem, "Alive" by Corrinne Clegg Hales (*Separate Escapes*, Ashland Poetry Press, 2002).

Amplifier. This poem is based on a conversation with lifelong friend, Bill Tuell, in his Fresno home. The recipe for this meat and cabbage pie is handed down in his family from a Volga German tradition of berrocks (sometimes referred to as bierocks or beerocks, though, as he would say, incorrectly).

Circumnavigating the Globe. Sidelights. A sailing ship would carry two of these between sunset and sunrise: one green, to starboard; one red, to port.

ACKNOWLEDGMENTS

I'm grateful to the editors and editorial staff at the following for all that you do to champion poetry, and for publishing versions of the following:

FUSION Magazine (Summer, 2022). "Sunflowers" and "Still Life in Wartime" as part of a hybrid essay, "The Word *Beauty* Within the Broken Instrument of the Body."

The New York Times' The Privacy Project (2020). "Alexa, Awake."

Poetry at Sangam (Sepember 2017 and January 2020). "The Bodies" (also published in the collaboration, *Four Faces of Loss*, with poets Sadek Mohammed, Mujib Merhdad, and Sholeh Wolpé by al-Wirsha, Baghdad, 2022), "Call It Leaves and Rain," "Molotov Cocktails," and "Vollum 14578" (with an earlier variation published in *My Life as a Foreign Country* by Jonathan Cape/Vintage in the U.K./W.W. Norton & Co. in the U.S.).

The Massachusetts Review (Volume 52, Issue 3 & 4). "Horses."

The Mighty Stream: Poems in Celebration of Martin Luther King. (Ed. by Carolyn Forché and Jackie Kay, Newcastle/Bloodaxe Poetry, 2017.) "Horses" and "The Buddhas of Bamiyan."

TriQuarterly (January 2017). "Twelve Roses for the Dead," as part of a roundtable essay curated by Tess Taylor (and developed from a panel she convened in 2017 with myself, Camille Dungy, Robert Polito, and Tom Sleigh).

★

I am *deeply* grateful to Carey Salerno for her belief in me and in the work I do, for her vision and guidance in this project from its earliest stages, and for her care in seeing each thing done right. Thank you to all at Alice James Books—both now and through the years—for your steadfast support of my work and for working so hard to see necessary voices take part in a larger poetic conversation now spanning fifty years. Many thanks to Julia Bouwsma for her fine-tuned attention to every word on the page. I'd also like to thank Anya Backlund at Blue Flower Arts for creating doorways into friendships and experiences that continually change my life for the better. And many thanks to Samar Hammam, at Rocking Chair Books, for that first phone call nearly twenty years ago, and for all the conversations since—your friendship and guidance (and wonderful eye in reading my manuscripts and offering advice) has seen me through the hardest of times.

As these manuscripts appeared, one draft to another, I leaned on the good hearts of these incredible writers and human beings with the hope that they might help the work in this trio of collections shine brighter—Laure-Anne Bosselaar, Nickole Brown, Stacey Lynn Brown, Samar Hammam, Patrick Hicks, Lee Herrick, Arthur Kusnetz, Peter Molin, June Sylvester Saraceno, and Christy Turner (who each read this work during the most trying of times). Thank you. Thank you. Thank you.

I'm grateful to Deborah Briggs and Jonathan Plutzik for residencies in The Writer's Room at The Betsy Hotel—a space commemorating the literary legacy of poet and veteran Hyam Plutzik. That rooftop view of the ocean helped me to clear my head and to see my way into several of the poems that appear in this book.

★

The album that accompanies this book (*Little Birds Singing*) was made possible by many kind-hearted souls and talented artists. A gift, each and every one.

Ilyse Kusnetz: vocals on 8, 9, 10.
Brian Voight: guitar on 10.

Brian Turner: vocals on all songs; bass on 1, 2, 3, 4, 8; guitar on 5, 6, 9, 10; flügelhorn 9.

Benjamin Kramer: bass on 1, 5, 6, 7; upright bass 8; keyboards on 1, 3; string arrangements on 1, 3.

Terri Kent: vocals on 1, 2, 3, 5, 6, 7.

Bill Tuell: guitar on 4 (music by Bill Tuell, lyrics by Brian Turner).

Christian Kiefer: drums on 4, 9; Mandolin 4.

Bobby Koelble: guitars on 3, 6, 10.

Damir Šodan: guitar on 9 (music by Damir Šodan and Brian Turner; lyrics by Brian Turner).

Corey Paul: trombone on 8.

Steve Woodward: drums on 4.

Josh Parsons: tuba solo 10.

Danny Jordan: flutes on 10.

Greg Parnell: drums on 8, 10.

Serena Kramer: piano on 1.

Connie Dawson: harp on 9.

Additional Vocals:

Skip Buhler 4/ Sarah Cossaboon 4, 9/ Chantal Thompson 4, 8/ Major Jackson 8, 9/ Didi Jackson 8, 9/ Stacey Lynn Brown 8, 10/ Marley Matejka 8, 10.

All tracks engineered, mixed, and mastered by Benjamin Kramer at 2Pi Creative Studios, Orlando, Florida—except:

Bill Tuell's guitars recorded by Eric Sherbon at Maximus Media, Inc., in Fresno, California (with thanks also to Ray Settle).

Terri Kent's vocals recorded by Michael Cox at Uprise Recording, in Sacramento, California.

★

I send my love and gratitude to Donald Anderson, Tony Barnstone, Jefferson Beavers, Shannon Beets, Jeff Bell, Kevin Bowen, Anitra Budd, Seth Brady Tucker, Gayle Brandeis, Skip Buhler, Camille Dungy, Rick Campbell, Pablo Cartaya, Matt Cashion, Brian Castner, Sophie Cherry, Steven Church, Russell Conrad, Shawn Crouch, Roel Daamen, Nana-Ama Danquah, Rupa DasGupta, Rob Deemer, Kurt and Heidi Erickson, Sarabjeet Garcha, Patsy Garoupa, Alison Granucci, Kelle Groom, Paul Guest, Nathalie Handal, Charles Hanzlicek, Alan Heathcock, Lisa Lee Herrick, Faylita Hicks, Garrett Hongo, Ashwani Kumar, Dorianne Laux, Kwang Ho Lee, Philip Levine, Rebecca Makkai, Tim Maxwell, Laura McCullough, Katie McDowell, Thomas McGuire, Mujib Merhdad, Dunya Mikhail, Joe Millar, Sadek Mohammed, Peter Mountford, Soheil Najm, Matt O'Donnell, Oliver de la Paz, Benjamin Percy, Susan Rich, Suzanne Roberts, Jake Runestad, John Schafer, Sean Sexton, Jared Silvia, Krystal Sital, Tess Taylor, Michael Thomas, Ernesto Trejo, Bill Tuell, Bruce Weigl, Sholeh Wolpé, Steven Woodward, Lidia Yuknavitch, and Arianne Zwartjes. Thank you for allowing me to be a part of your phenomenal lives. One of my deep regrets is in not adequately expressing how grateful I am to each of you.

To Corrinne Clegg Hales—I was the shy kid at the back of the class with the profound stammer, and I'll always be grateful for your encouragement and for all that you taught me about the art itself. Thank you for your friendship and mentorship over the years, Connie.

To Patrick Hicks—With every draft and revision, you've been there as my first reader. It's been an unspoken thing, a gift of such profound magnitude, and always with a keen eye to the art itself, while—at a deeper level—helping me as I attempt to write my way into the rest of my life.

To Stacey Lynn Brown—Through the highs and lows that years and decades bring, you remain a constant friend through it all. It's been a gift to be a part of your life. Remember—if you find yourself in a bar fight (which I don't recommend), don't worry, I got your back (and I'll hold your drink).

To Benjamin Busch—Thanks for keeping me upright and steady in the low times, man, and for hitting the high notes that remind us all that Rock is not dead.

To June Sylvester Saraceno—Thanks for being the gift of a sister I met late in a life. I'll meet you at the river with Luna and Dene! Thank you for always being there for me.

I send my abiding love to friends and family, loved ones all, both near and far.

★

Ilyse—my love to you, always—
    I'll meet you at the door we framed with stars

RECENT TITLES FROM ALICE JAMES BOOKS

The Goodbye World Poem, Brian Turner
The Wild Delight of Wild Things, Brian Turner
I Am the Most Dangerous Thing, Candace Williams
Burning Like Her Own Planet, Vandana Khanna
Standing in the Forest of Being Alive, Katie Farris
Feast, Ina Cariño
Decade of the Brain: Poems, Janine Joseph
American Treasure, Jill McDonough
We Borrowed Gentleness, J. Estanislao Lopez
Brother Sleep, Aldo Amparán
Sugar Work, Katie Marya
Museum of Objects Burned by the Souls in Purgatory, Jeffrey Thomson
Constellation Route, Matthew Olzmann
How to Not Be Afraid of Everything, Jane Wong
Brocken Spectre, Jacques J. Rancourt
No Ruined Stone, Shara McCallum
The Vault, Andrés Cerpa
White Campion, Donald Revell
Last Days, Tamiko Beyer
If This Is the Age We End Discovery, Rosebud Ben-Oni
Pretty Tripwire, Alessandra Lynch
Inheritance, Taylor Johnson
The Voice of Sheila Chandra, Kazim Ali
Arrow, Sumita Chakraborty
Country, Living, Ira Sadoff
Hot with the Bad Things, Lucia LoTempio
Witch, Philip Matthews

Alice James Books is committed to publishing books that matter. The press was founded in 1973 in Boston, Massachusetts to give women access to publishing. As a cooperative, authors performed the day-to-day undertakings of the press. The press continues to expand and grow from its formative roots, guided by its founding values of access, excellence, inclusivity, and collaboration in publishing. Its mission is to publish books that matter and preserve a place of belonging for poets who inspire us. AJB seeks to broaden our collective interpretation of what constitutes the American poetic voice and is dedicated to helping its artists achieve purposeful engagement with broad audiences and communities nationwide. The press was named for Alice James, sister to William and Henry, whose extraordinary gift for writing went unrecognized during her lifetime.

Designed by Alban Fischer

Printed by Sheridan Saline